C0 3 74 95528 93

THE SCIENCE OF
FOOTBALL

By
Emilie Dufresne

PLAY
SMART

BookLife
PUBLISHING

©2019
BookLife Publishing
King's Lynn
Norfolk PE30 4LS

ISBN: 978-1-78637-530-8

Written by:
Emilie Dufresne

Edited by:
Kirsty Holmes

Designed by:
Gareth Liddington

Photocredits:

Cover – Fotokostic, Taweesak Jaroensin, irin-k, matthew25, Agustin Vai, 9dream studio, Alexander Mak. 2 - Volodymyr Kyrylyuk. 4 - Monkey Business Images. 5 - Fotokostic. 6 - Pressmaster. 7 - Pressmaster. 8 - Monkey Business Images. 9 - Roka Pics. 10 - nexus7. 12 - nektofadeev. 13 - Paolo Bona. 14 - Alexander Kochkin. 15 - Creativa Images. 16 - Matt Trommer. 17 - Gino Santa Maria. 18 - Laszlo Szirtesi. 19 - ostill. 20 - Fotokostic. 21 - Natursports. 23 - Natursports.

Images are courtesy of Shutterstock.com. With thanks to Getty Images, Thinkstock Photo and iStockphoto.

CONTENTS

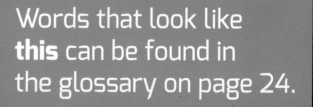

Words that look like **this** can be found in the glossary on page 24.

KICK-OFF!

Are you ready to learn all about the **forces**, angles and energy behind football? Then put on your shin pads and pull up your socks; the game is about to kick off!

Each football team has 11 players. Two teams play against each other and try to get the ball in the other team's goal.

ARE YOU READY?

THEN LET'S GET ON THE PITCH!

CAN YOU KICK IT?

THE FORCE OF THE KICK IS SPREAD ACROSS THE BALL.

THE BALL WILL FOLLOW THE DIRECTION YOUR FOOT IS FACING.

BECAUSE THE FORCE IS SPREAD OUT, THE BALL WON'T TRAVEL VERY FAST.

Kicking the ball with the side of your foot spreads the force across the ball. This type of shot is not very **powerful**, but is very **accurate**.

When you kick the ball with your toe, the force of the kick is focused in one place. This kick is strong and fast, but less accurate.

THE BALL WILL FOLLOW THE DIRECTION OF YOUR KICK.

THE FORCE OF THE KICK IS DIRECTED HERE.

FAST KICKS WILL CREATE MORE FORCE.

HOW TO HEADER

When the ball is travelling in the air, it has a lot of force pushing it in the direction it is travelling.

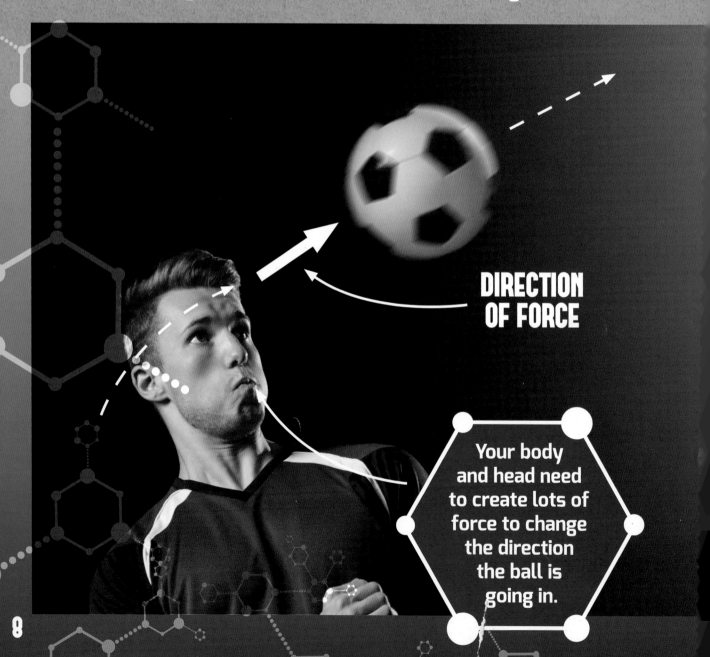

DIRECTION OF FORCE

Your body and head need to create lots of force to change the direction the ball is going in.

Curving your back and jumping before heading the ball will build up **momentum** in your body.

MOMENTUM FROM CURVING BODY

BALL FORCED TO CHANGE DIRECTION

When you header the ball, the energy built up in your body will force the ball in a different direction.

BEND THE BALL

Bending the ball in the air can be useful for getting around tricky **opponents**. Instead of travelling in a straight line, the ball curves in the air.

LEFT-FOOTED? STAND TO THE RIGHT OF THE BALL AND KICK THE BOTTOM LEFT HAND CORNER.

RIGHT-FOOTED? STAND TO THE LEFT OF THE BALL AND KICK THE BOTTOM RIGHT HAND CORNER.

Kicking the ball off-centre means that it will spin.
The spinning of the ball changes how it moves in the air.

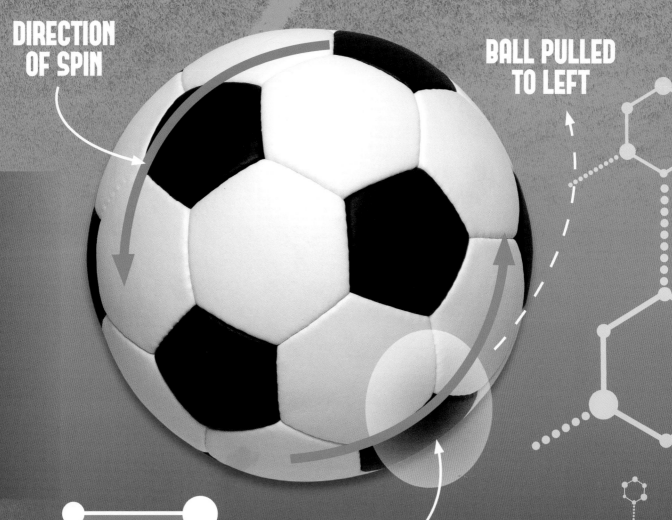

DIRECTION OF SPIN

BALL PULLED TO LEFT

KICKED HERE

The air moves quicker in the direction the ball is spinning. This pulls the ball away from the direction that it was kicked.

Twist your shoulders to get even more curve on the ball.

CRACKING CORNERS

Know which player you want to pass the ball to, so that you know which angle to kick the ball at.

Corner kicks are all about giving your team the best **opportunity** to score a goal. These **crosses** are less about force and more about being accurate.

You also need to think about how far away the player is and how it is best to get the ball to them.

In this situation, the player needs to get the ball up and over the defenders.

He will need to scoop the ball upwards and with a lot of force to get far enough over the opponents.

CHAMPION OF CHEST CONTROL

If the ball is moving high and fast towards you, you can try and control it using your chest.

ABSORB SOME OF THE FORCE OF THE BALL BY LEANING BACK AS IT COMES TO YOU.

FORCE OF BALL

ARCH YOUR BACK TO CUSHION THE BALL.

This will allow the force of the ball to spread across your chest, instead of bouncing the ball off you.

Because the force of the ball has been spread across your chest, the ball has no energy or momentum pushing it in any direction. The largest force acting on the ball now is gravity.

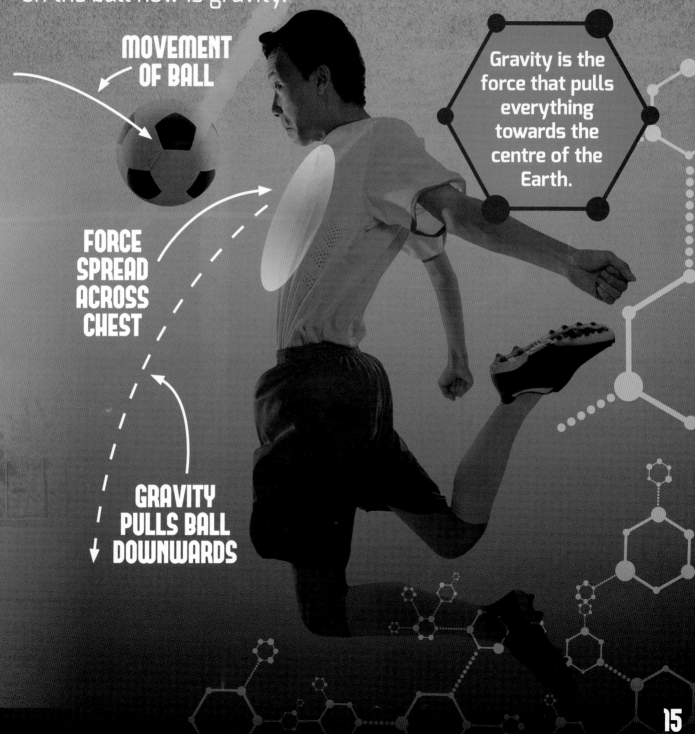

MOVEMENT OF BALL

FORCE SPREAD ACROSS CHEST

GRAVITY PULLS BALL DOWNWARDS

Gravity is the force that pulls everything towards the centre of the Earth.

BRAVE A BICYCLE KICK

This builds up more momentum in your leg than you could get from a normal kick.

To perfect a bicycle kick, you need to go against gravity and jump up in the air, then swing your leg 180° or more up towards the ball to kick it behind you.

The momentum built up in your leg is transferred to the ball when you kick it. This makes the ball travel harder and faster than any other kick.

BALL FORCED BEHIND YOU

MOMENTUM FROM SWING

GRAVITY PULLS YOUR BODY DOWNWARDS

PUNCH IT AWAY

Goalkeepers need to clear the ball from near the goal. They do this by blocking, catching, diving and punching.

To punch the ball away, you need to build up lots of energy in your body to stop the ball moving into the goal and push it in a different direction.

Jumping and pushing your arms outwards will build up momentum in your body.

ENERGY IS TRANSFERRED FROM YOUR LEGS AND ARMS AND IS PUSHED INTO THE BALL.

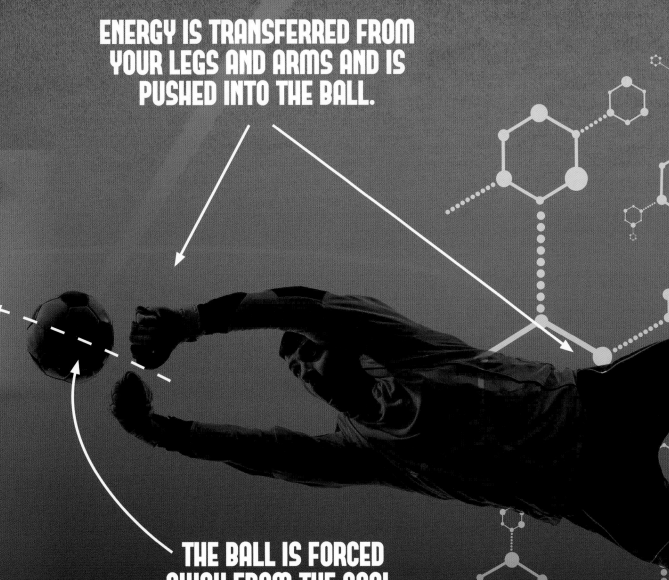

THE BALL IS FORCED AWAY FROM THE GOAL.

SAVE IT!

To make a save, you need to be able to **predict** where the ball is going. Knowing the different moves in this book will help you be a great goalkeeper.

This keeper knew the path the ball would take. This meant he could get in the right position to save it.

Try and save this strike! Using the knowledge you have learnt from this book, where do you think the ball is going in this picture? Is it number 1, 2 or 3?

Don't forget that the player might be curving the ball!

SPOT THE BALL

That's right, it's number 3! Let's take a closer look at the science behind the shot.

BODY TWIST

This player has twisted their body around the ball. This suggests that they will be playing a shot that curves in the air around the keeper.

POSITION OF FOOT

The inside of this player's right foot will hit the bottom right side of the ball. This will scoop the ball up and around in the air.

DIRECTION OF CURVE

Instead of kicking the ball directly to the keeper, the ball will curve out and around the keeper.

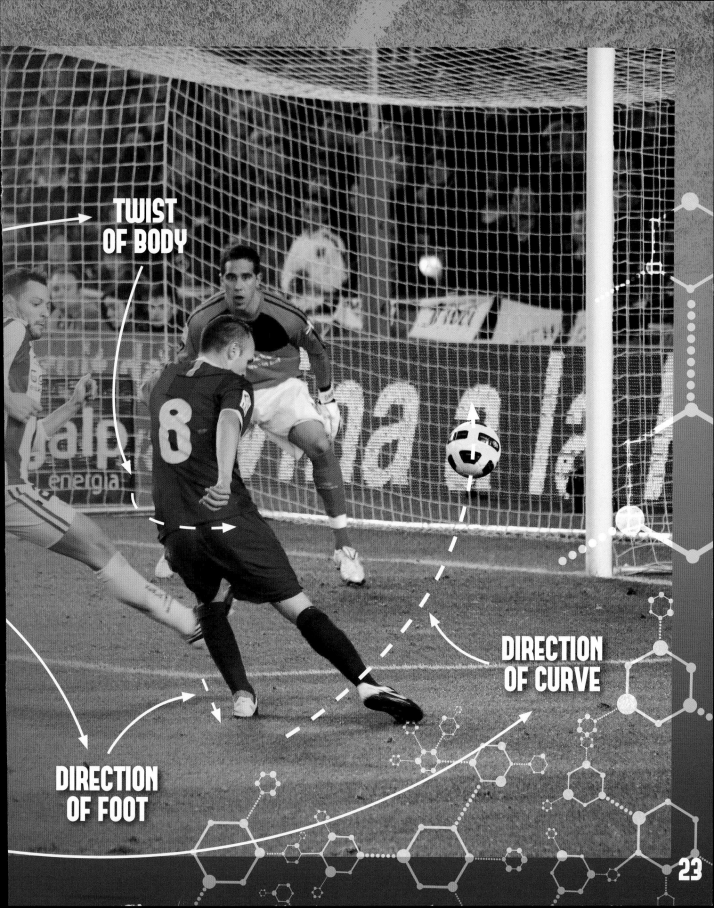

TWIST
OF BODY

DIRECTION
OF CURVE

DIRECTION
OF FOOT

GLOSSARY

absorb	to reduce the force of
accurate	precise and on target
crosses	a mid to long pass from near the edge of the pitch into the centre near the opponents' goal
cushion	to soften the effect of something
forces	a push or pull on an object
momentum	how fast an object is moving because of its speed and weight
opponents	members of the team playing against you
opportunity	given the chance
powerful	having lots of power or strength
predict	to guess what will happen

INDEX